Hal•Leonard

BLUES PLAY-ALONG

Book & CD for B♭, E♭, Bass Clef and C instruments

VOLUME 2

TEXAS BLUES

PLAY 8 SONGS WITH A ~~~~~~ BAND

HOW TO USE THE CD:

Each song has <u>two</u> tracks:

1) Full Stereo Mix

All recorded instruments are present on this track.

2) Split Track

Piano and **Bass** parts can be removed
by turning down the volume on the LEFT channel.

Guitar, Harp, and **Horn** parts can be removed
by turning down the volume on the RIGHT channel.

ISBN 978-1-4234-5348-2

HAL•LEONARD®
CORPORATION

7777 W. BLUEMOUND RD. P.O. BOX 13819 MILWAUKEE, WI 53213

Visit Hal Leonard Online at
www.halleonard.com

TEXAS BLUES

CD TRACK

① Full Stereo Mix

⑨ Split Mix

C Version

Hide Away

By Freddie King and Sonny Thompson

Medium Fast Shuffle ♩ = 138

4

STRAIGHT 8THS (♫ = ♫)

⊕ CODA **STRAIGHT 8THS** (♫ = ♫)

If You Love Me Like You Say

Words and Music by Little Johnny Taylor

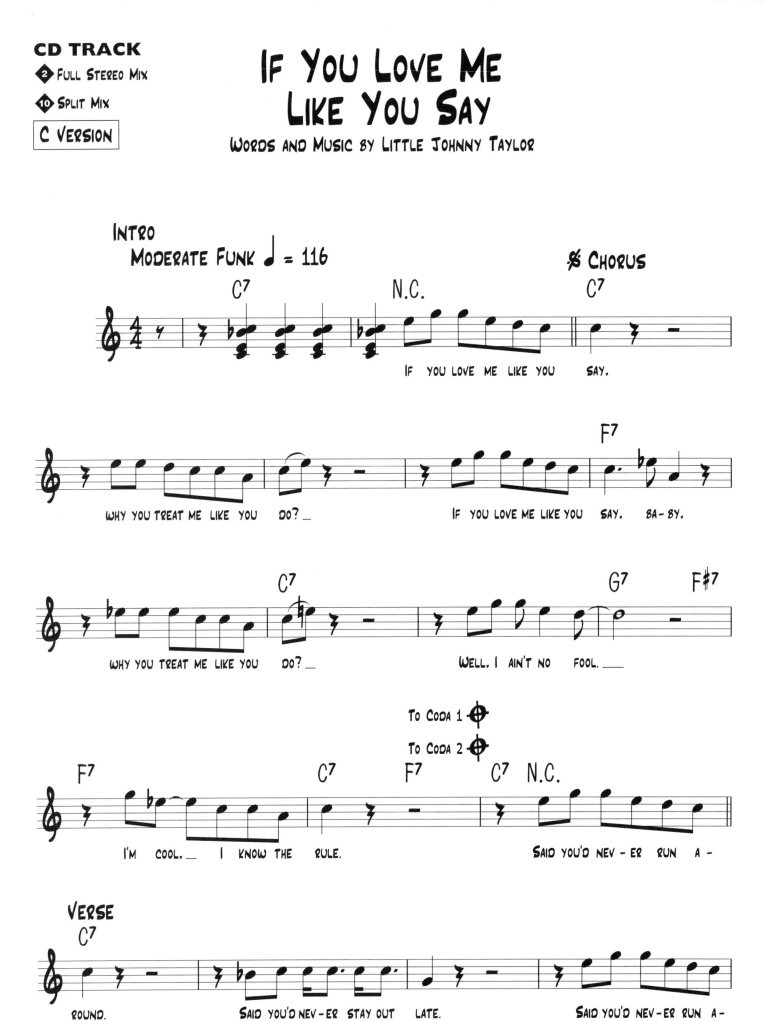

ROUND, BA-BY. SAID YOU'D NEV-ER STAY OUT LATE. LET ME TELL YOU, PERT-TY

BABE. I'VE GOT ___ TO SET YOU STRAIGHT. IF YOU LOVE ME LIKE YOU

⊕ CODA 1

GUITAR/HARP SOLOS

1.-4. | 5. D.S. AL CODA 2

IF YOU LOVE ME LIKE YOU

⊕ CODA 2

OUTRO

WHY ___ YAH, YAH YAH.

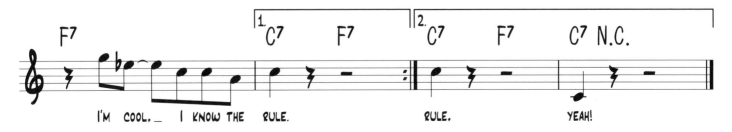

I'M COOL, ___ I KNOW THE RULE. RULE, YEAH!

Mojo Hand

Words and Music by
Morris Levy, Sam Hopkins and Clarence L. Lewis

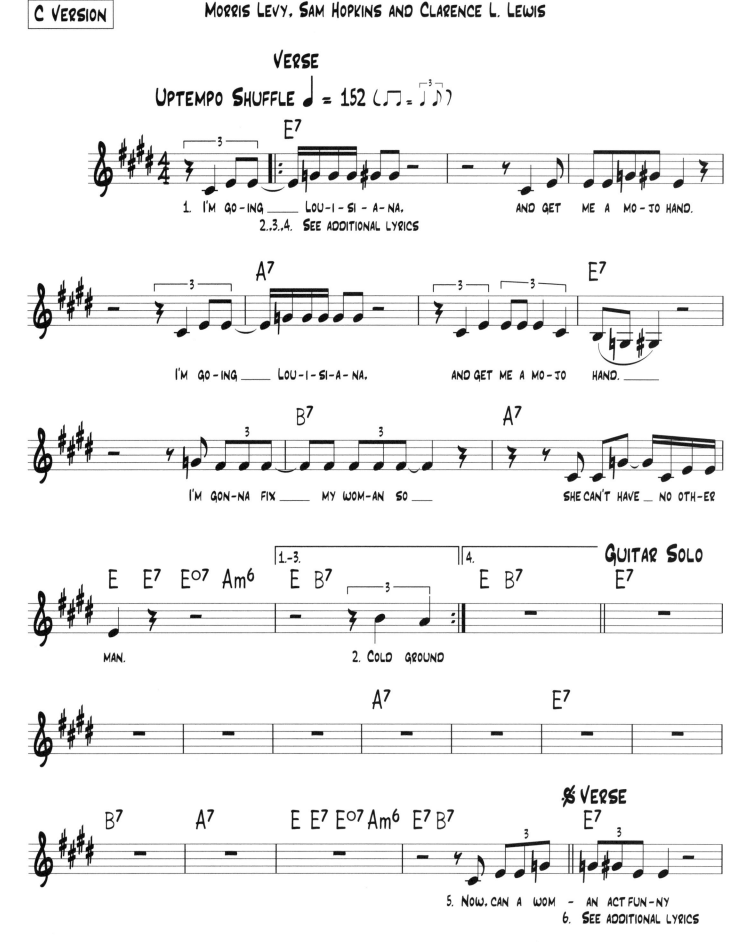

WHEN SHE GOT AN-OTH-ER MAN? CAN A WOM-AN ACT FUN-NY ___

WHEN SHE GOT AN-OTH-ER MAN? YOU KNOW SHE WON'T LOOK STRAIGHT AT YOU,

THEN SHE'S AL-WAYS RAIS-IN' SAND.

6. WELL, I'M GO-IN' TO -

ADDITIONAL LYRICS

2. COLD GROUND WAS MY BED LAST NIGHT, ROCKS WAS MY PILLOW, TOO.
COLD GROUND WAS MY BED LAST NIGHT, ROCKS WAS MY PILLOW, TOO.
I WOKE UP THIS MORNIN', I WONDERED, "WHAT IN THE WORLD AM I GONNA DO?"

3. I LAY DOWN THINKIN', "BUY ME A MOJO HAND."
I LAY DOWN THINKIN', "BUY ME A MOJO HAND."
I JUST WANNA FIX MY WOMAN SO SHE CAN'T HAVE NO OTHER MAN.

4. BUT DON'T LET YOUR WOMAN FIX YOU LIKE MINE FIXED ME.
DON'T LET YOUR WOMAN, BOY, FIX YOU LIKE MINE FIXED ME.
SHE MAKE A FOOL ABOUT HER, ABOUT AS A FOOL CAN BE.

6. WELL, I'M GOIN' TOMORROW, BUT I WON'T BE GONE LONG.
I'M GOIN' TOMORROW, BUT I WON'T BE GONE VERY LONG.
I'M GONNA GET ME A MOJO HAND, I'M GONNA BRING IT BACK HOME.

Okie Dokie Stomp

Words and Music by Plummer "Ivory" Davis

Fast Blues Shuffle ♩ = 182

%. Guitar Solo

To Coda ⊕

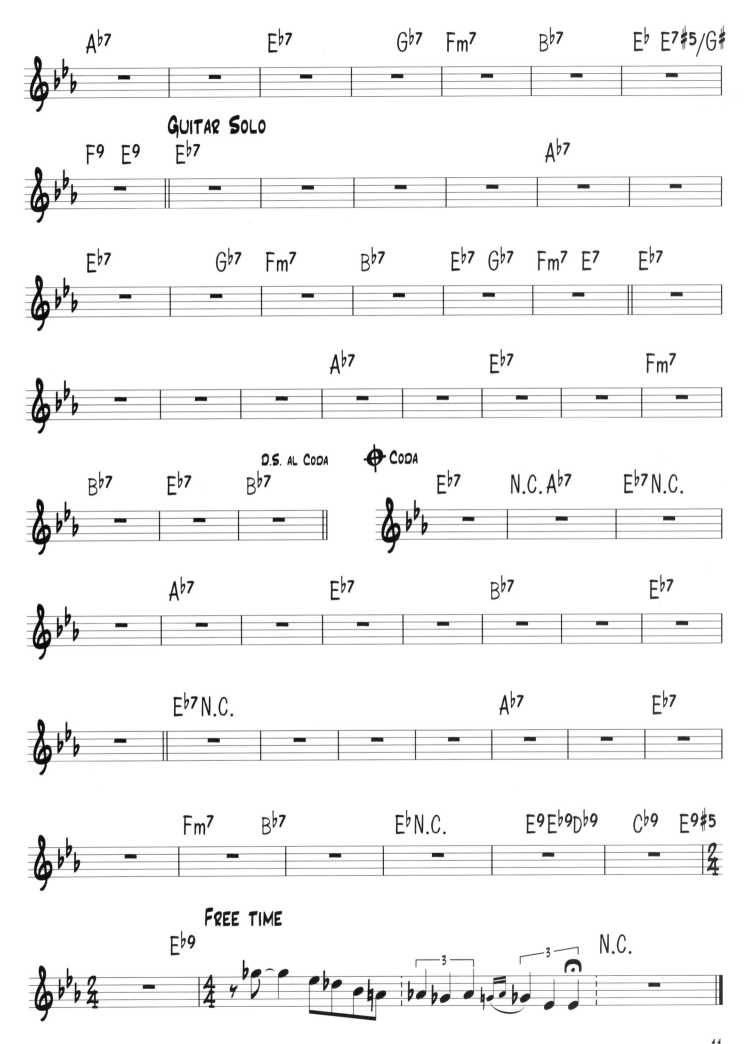

CD TRACK
⑤ Full Stereo Mix
⑬ Split Mix

C Version

Pride and Joy
Written by Stevie Ray Vaughan

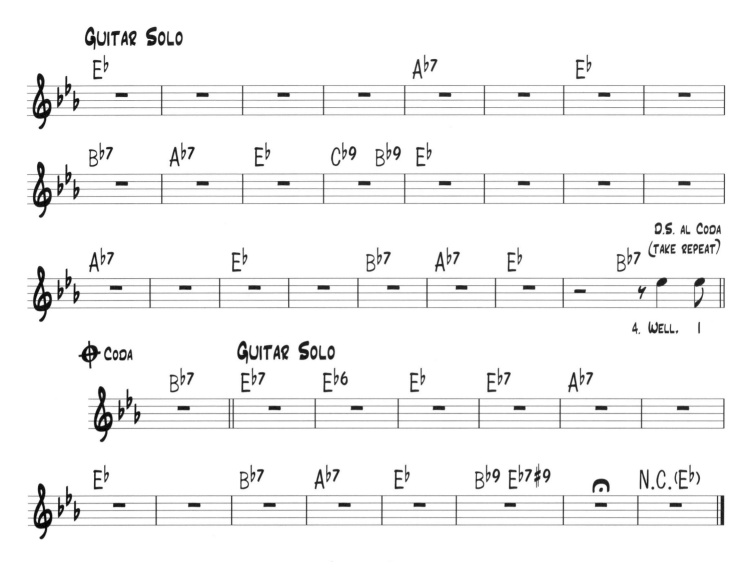

Additional Lyrics

2. Yeah, I love my baby, my heart and soul.
   Love like ours ah, won't never grow old.
   She('s) me sweet little thang,
   She('s) my pride and joy.
   She('s) my sweet little baby,
   I'm her little lover boy.

3. Yeah, I love my lady to be long and lean.
   You mess with her, you'll see a man gettin' mean.
   She('s) my sweet little thang,
   She('s) my pride and joy.
   She('s) my sweet little baby,
   I'm her little lover boy.

4. Well, I love my baby like the finest w. wine.
   Stick with her until the end of time.
   An' she's my sweet little thang,
   She('s) my pride and joy.
   She('s) my sweet little baby,
   I'm her little lover boy.

5. Yeah, I love my baby, my heart and soul.
   Love like ours ah, won't never grow old.
   She('s) my sweet little thang,
   She('s) my pride and joy.
   She('s) my sweet little baby,
   I'm her little lover boy.

CD TRACK

6 Full Stereo Mix

14 Split Mix

C Version

Reconsider Baby

Words and Music by Lowell Fulson

C7　　　　　　G7

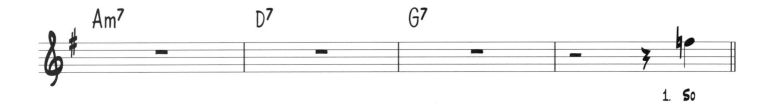

Am7　　　　D7　　　　G7

1. So

𝄋 Verse

LONG, _____　　OH, HOW I HATE __ TO SEE YOU GO.

2., 3. See additional lyrics

SO LONG, _____　　OH, HOW I HATE __ TO SEE YOU

GO. AND THE WAY THAT I WILL MISS YOU, ___

To Coda

I GUESS YOU WILL NEV - ER KNOW.

2. WE'VE BEEN TO-GETH-

HARP/GUITAR SOLOS

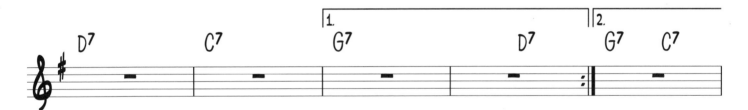

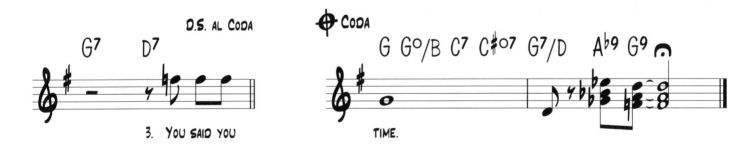

D.S. AL CODA

3. YOU SAID YOU

Coda

TIME.

ADDITIONAL LYRICS

2. WE'VE BEEN TOGETHER SO LONG TO HAVE TO SEPARATE THIS WAY.
   WE'VE BEEN TOGETHER SO LONG TO HAVE TO SEPARATE THIS WAY.
   I'M GONNA LET YOU GO AHEAD ON, BABY, PRAY THAT YOU'LL COME BACK HOME SOME DAY.

3. YOU SAID YOU ONCE HAD LOVED ME, BUT NOW I GUESS YOU HAVE CHANGED YOUR MIND.
   YOU SAID YOU ONCE HAD LOVED ME, BUT NOW I GUESS YOU HAVE CHANGED YOUR MIND.
   WHY DON'T YOU RECONSIDER, BABY, GIVE YOURSELF JUST A LITTLE MORE TIME.

CD TRACK

7 Full Stereo Mix

15 Split Mix

C Version

T-Bone Shuffle
By T-Bone Walker

Intro

Uptempo Shuffle ♩ = 138

Harp/Guitar Solos

Additional Lyrics

2. You can't take it with you, that's one thing for sure.
   You can't take it with you, that's one thing for sure.
   There's nothing wrong with you that a good shuffle boogie won't cure.

3. Have your fun while you can, fate's an awful thing.
   Have your fun while you can, fate's an awful thing.
   You can't tell what might happen, that's why I love to sing.

The Things That I Used to Do

Words and Music by Eddie "Guitar Slim" Jones

GUITAR SOLO

F   B♭   F   F7

B♭   F   F7

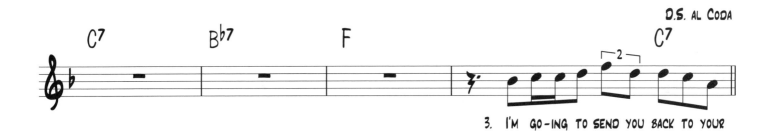

D.S. AL CODA

C7   B♭7   F   C7

3. I'M GO-ING TO SEND YOU BACK TO YOUR

⊕ CODA

OUTRO
STRAIGHT 8THS (♫ = ♫)

F6   B♭7   B°7   F6/C   G♭7   F7

ADDITIONAL LYRICS

2. I WOULD SEARCH ALL NIGHT FOR YOU, BABY,
   LORD, AND MY SEARCH WOULD ALWAYS END IN VAIN.
   I WOULD SEARCH ALL NIGHT FOR YOU, BABY,
   LORD, AND MY SEARCH WOULD ALWAYS END IN VAIN.
   BUT I KNEW ALL ALONG, DARLIN',
   THAT YOU WAS HID OUT WITH YOUR OTHER MAN.

3. I'M GOING TO SEND YOU BACK TO YOUR MOTHER, BABY,
   LORD, AND I'M GOING BACK TO MY FAMILY, TOO.
   I'M GOING TO SEND YOU BACK TO YOUR MOTHER, BABY,
   LORD, AND I'M GOING BACK TO MY FAMILY, TOO.
   'CAUSE NOTHIN' I DO THAT PLEASE YOU, BABY,
   LORD, I JUST CAN'T GET ALONG WITH YOU.

Hide Away

By Freddie King and Sonny Thompson

Bb Version

Medium Fast Shuffle ♩ = 138

To Coda ⊕

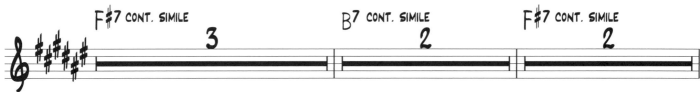

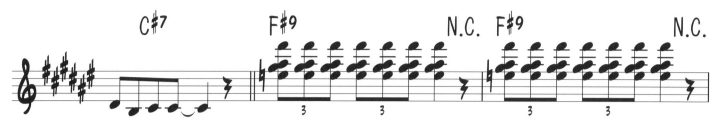

STRAIGHT 8THS (♩♩ = ♩♩)

✛ CODA   **STRAIGHT 8THS** (♩♩ = ♩♩)

If You Love Me Like You Say
Words and Music by Little Johnny Taylor

ROUND, BA-BY. SAID YOU'D NEV-ER STAY OUT LATE. LET ME TELL YOU, PERT-TY

D.S. AL CODA 1

BABE. I'VE GOT ___ TO SET YOU STRAIGHT. IF YOU LOVE ME LIKE YOU

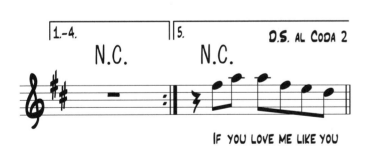

✛ CODA 1

GUITAR/HARP SOLOS

✛ CODA 2

OUTRO

D.S. AL CODA 2

1.-4. / 5.

IF YOU LOVE ME LIKE YOU

WHY _ YAH, YAH YAH.

I'M COOL, _ I KNOW THE RULE. RULE, YEAH!

Mojo Hand

Words and Music by
Morris Levy, Sam Hopkins and Clarence L. Lewis

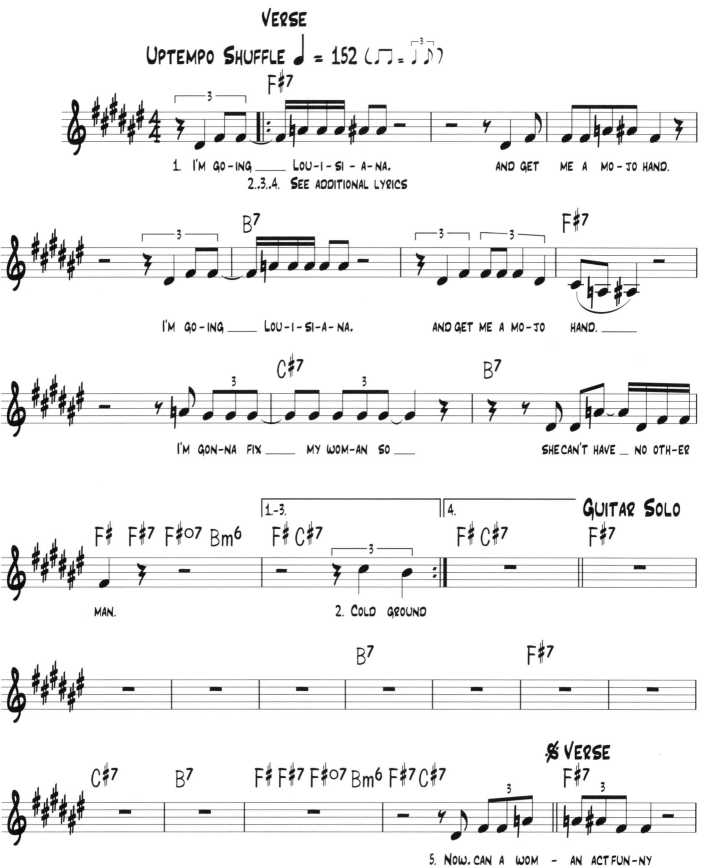

To Coda ⊕

Harp Solo

D.S. al Coda

⊕ **Coda**

WHEN SHE GOT AN-OTH-ER MAN?

CAN A WOM-AN ACT FUN-NY ___

WHEN SHE GOT AN-OTH-ER MAN?

YOU KNOW SHE WON'T LOOK STRAIGHT AT YOU.

THEN SHE'S AL-WAYS RAIS-IN' SAND.

6. WELL, I'M GO-IN' TO -

Additional Lyrics

2. COLD GROUND WAS MY BED LAST NIGHT, ROCKS WAS MY PILLOW, TOO.
   COLD GROUND WAS MY BED LAST NIGHT, ROCKS WAS MY PILLOW, TOO.
   I WOKE UP THIS MORNIN', I WONDERED, "WHAT IN THE WORLD AM I GONNA DO?"

3. I LAY DOWN THINKIN', "BUY ME A MOJO HAND."
   I LAY DOWN THINKIN', "BUY ME A MOJO HAND."
   I JUST WANNA FIX MY WOMAN SO SHE CAN'T HAVE NO OTHER MAN.

4. BUT DON'T LET YOUR WOMAN FIX YOU LIKE MINE FIXED ME.
   DON'T LET YOUR WOMAN, BOY, FIX YOU LIKE MINE FIXED ME.
   SHE MAKE A FOOL ABOUT HER, ABOUT AS A FOOL CAN BE.

6. WELL, I'M GOIN' TOMORROW, BUT I WON'T BE GONE LONG.
   I'M GOIN' TOMORROW, BUT I WON'T BE GONE VERY LONG.
   I'M GONNA GET ME A MOJO HAND, I'M GONNA BRING IT BACK HOME.

Okie Dokie Stomp

Words and Music by Plummer "Ivory" Davis

Fast Blues Shuffle ♩ = 182

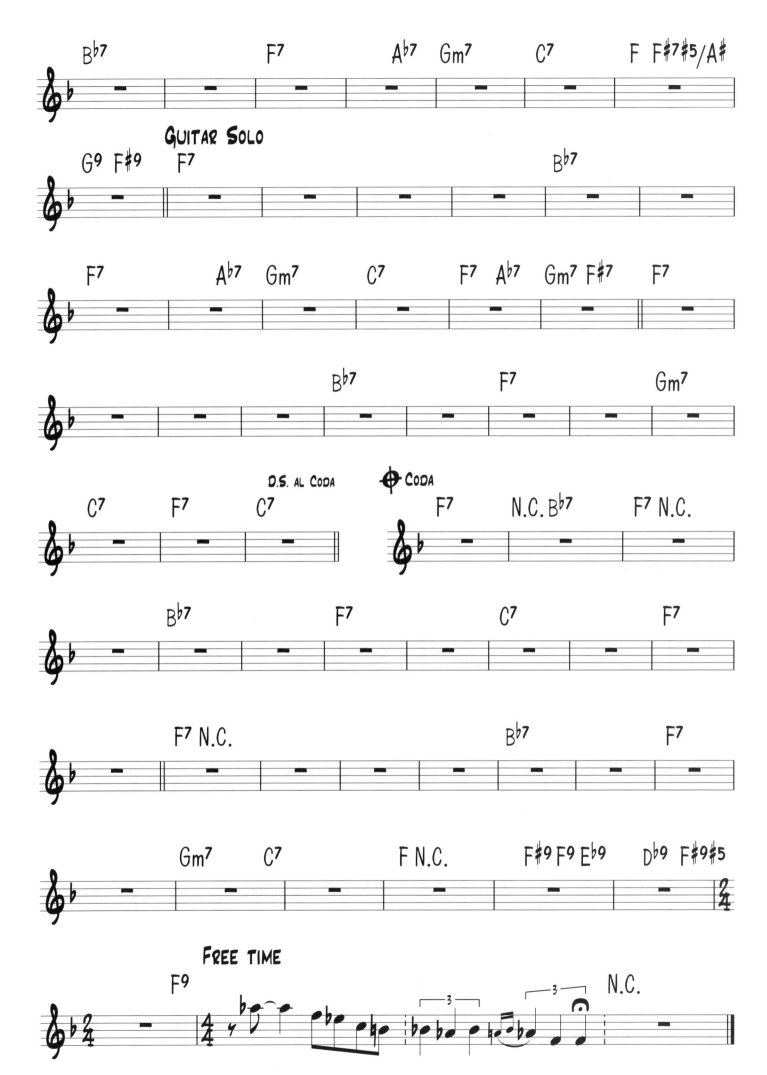

PRIDE AND JOY
WRITTEN BY STEVIE RAY VAUGHAN

Bb VERSION

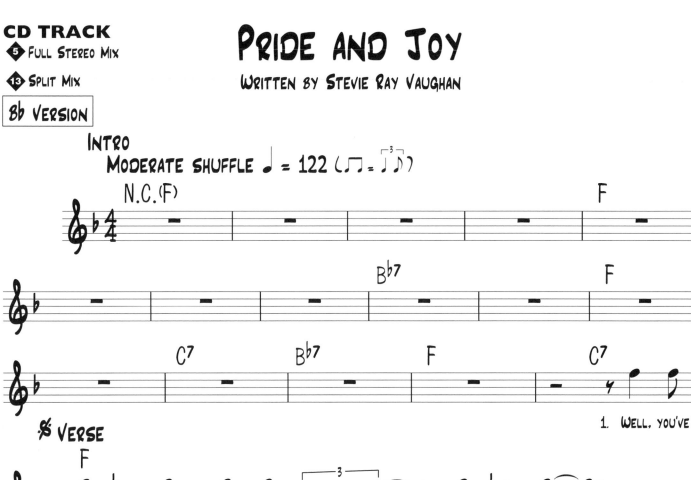

INTRO
MODERATE SHUFFLE ♩ = 122

HEARD A - BOUT LOV - IN' GIV - IN' SIGHT ___ TO THE BLIND. ___
2., 3., 4., 5. SEE ADDITIONAL LYRICS

MY BA - BY'S LOV - IN' 'CAUSE THE SUN ___ TO SHINE. ___ AN' SHE'S MY

SWEET ___ LIT - TLE THANG. ___ SHE('S) MY PRIDE AND JOY. ___

SHE('S) ___ MY SWEET LIT - TLE BA - BY, I'M ___

___ HER ___ LIT - TLE LOV - ER BOY. ___ 2. YEAH, I

1. WELL, YOU'VE

TO CODA

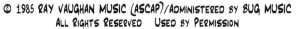

ADDITIONAL LYRICS

2. YEAH, I LOVE MY BABY, MY HEART AND SOUL.
LOVE LIKE OURS AH, WON'T NEVER GROW OLD.
SHE('S) ME SWEET LITTLE THANG,
SHE('S) MY PRIDE AND JOY.
SHE('S) MY SWEET LITTLE BABY,
I'M HER LITTLE LOVER BOY.

3. YEAH, I LOVE MY LADY TO BE LONG AND LEAN,
YOU MESS WITH HER, YOU'LL SEE A MAN GETTIN' MEAN.
SHE('S) MY SWEET LITTLE THANG.
SHE('S) MY PRIDE AND JOY.
SHE('S) MY SWEET LITTLE BABY,
I'M HER LITTLE LOVER BOY.

4. WELL, I LOVE MY BABY LIKE THE FINEST W, WINE.
STICK WITH HER UNTIL THE END OF TIME.
AN' SHE'S MY SWEET LITTLE THANG,
SHE('S) MY PRIDE AND JOY.
SHE('S) MY SWEET LITTLE BABY,
I'M HER LITTLE LOVER BOY.

5. YEAH, I LOVE MY BABY, MY HEART AND SOUL.
LOVE LIKE OURS AH, WON'T NEVER GROW OLD.
SHE('S) MY SWEET LITTLE THANG,
SHE('S) MY PRIDE AND JOY.
SHE('S) MY SWEET LITTLE BABY,
I'M HER LITTLE LOVER BOY.

Reconsider Baby
Words and Music by Lowell Fulson

INTRO-SOLO
MODERATE SHUFFLE ♩ = 96

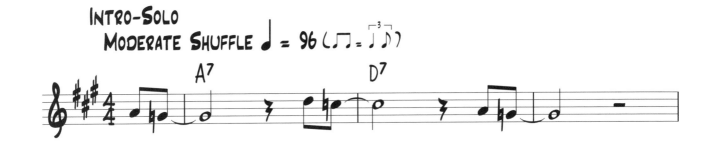

1. So

%. VERSE

LONG, _____
2., 3. See additional lyrics

OH, HOW I HATE __ TO SEE YOU GO.

So LONG, _____

OH, HOW I HATE __ TO SEE YOU

GO.   AND THE WAY THAT I WILL MISS YOU. ___

I GUESS YOU WILL NEV - ER KNOW.   2. WE'VE BEEN TO-GETH-

HARP/GUITAR SOLOS

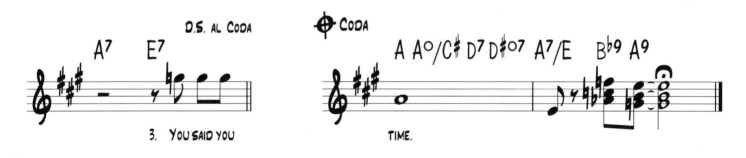

3. YOU SAID YOU   TIME.

ADDITIONAL LYRICS

2. WE'VE BEEN TOGETHER SO LONG TO HAVE TO SEPARATE THIS WAY.
   WE'VE BEEN TOGETHER SO LONG TO HAVE TO SEPARATE THIS WAY.
   I'M GONNA LET YOU GO AHEAD ON, BABY, PRAY THAT YOU'LL COME BACK HOME SOME DAY.

3. YOU SAID YOU ONCE HAD LOVED ME, BUT NOW I GUESS YOU HAVE CHANGED YOUR MIND.
   YOU SAID YOU ONCE HAD LOVED ME, BUT NOW I GUESS YOU HAVE CHANGED YOUR MIND.
   WHY DON'T YOU RECONSIDER, BABY, GIVE YOURSELF JUST A LITTLE MORE TIME.

T-Bone Shuffle
By T-Bone Walker

Intro
Uptempo Shuffle ♩ = 138

A⁶

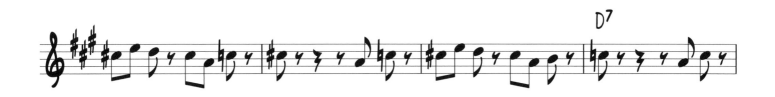

D⁷

A⁶   E⁹

Harp/Guitar Solos
A⁶

D⁷   A⁶

D⁷

A⁶   Bm⁷   E⁹   A⁶

Additional Lyrics

2. You can't take it with you, that's one thing for sure.
   You can't take it with you, that's one thing for sure.
   There's nothing wrong with you that a good shuffle boogie won't cure.

3. Have your fun while you can, fate's an awful thing.
   Have your fun while you can, fate's an awful thing.
   You can't tell what might happen, that's why I love to sing.

The Things That I Used to Do

Words and Music by Eddie "Guitar Slim" Jones

%% Verse

Slow Shuffle ♩. = 63

1. The things that I used to do,   Lord,_ I won't do _____ NO
2., 3. See additional lyrics

MORE.   The things that I used to do,

Lord,_ I won't do _____ no   more.

I used to sit and hold your hand, ba - by,   CRY, _____ beg-gin' you not to go. _

To Coda ⊕

1.   D7   2.

Guitar Solo

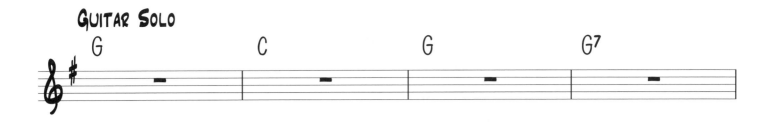

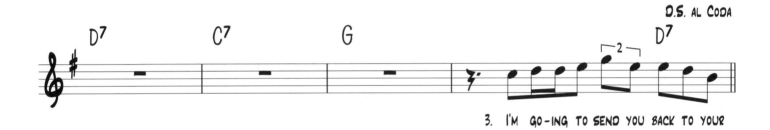

D.S. al Coda

3.   I'm go-ing to send you back to your

Coda
Outro
Straight 8ths

Additional Lyrics

2. I would search all night for you, baby,
    Lord, and my search would always end in vain.
    I would search all night for you, baby,
    Lord, and my search would always end in vain.
    But I knew all along, darlin',
    That you was hid out with your other man.

3. I'm going to send you back to your mother, baby,
    Lord, and I'm going back to my family, too.
    I'm going to send you back to your mother, baby,
    Lord, and I'm going back to my family, too.
    'Cause nothin' I do that please you, baby,
    Lord, I just can't get along with you.

Hide Away

By Freddie King and Sonny Thompson

Eb Version

Medium Fast Shuffle ♩ = 138

To Coda ⊕

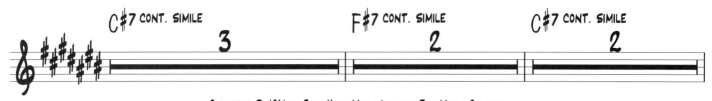

STRAIGHT 8THS (♪♩ = ♩♪)

D.S. AL CODA

⊕ CODA   STRAIGHT 8THS (♪♩ = ♪♪)

If You Love Me Like You Say

Words and Music by Little Johnny Taylor

ROUND, BA-BY.   SAID YOU'D NEV-ER STAY OUT   LATE.   LET ME TELL YOU, PERT-TY

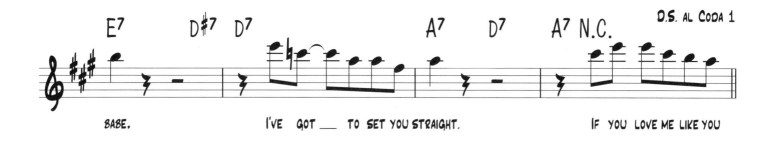

D.S. AL CODA 1

BABE.   I'VE GOT ___ TO SET YOU STRAIGHT.   IF YOU LOVE ME LIKE YOU

⊕ CODA 1

GUITAR/HARP SOLOS

⊕ CODA 2

OUTRO

IF YOU LOVE ME LIKE YOU   WHY _ YAH, YAH   YAH.

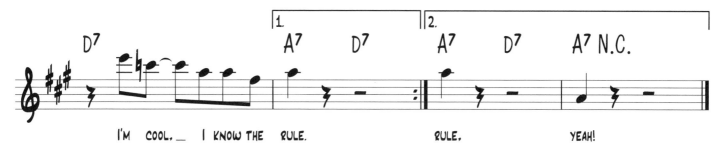

I'M COOL.__ I KNOW THE RULE.   RULE.   YEAH!

Mojo Hand

Words and Music by
Morris Levy, Sam Hopkins and Clarence L. Lewis

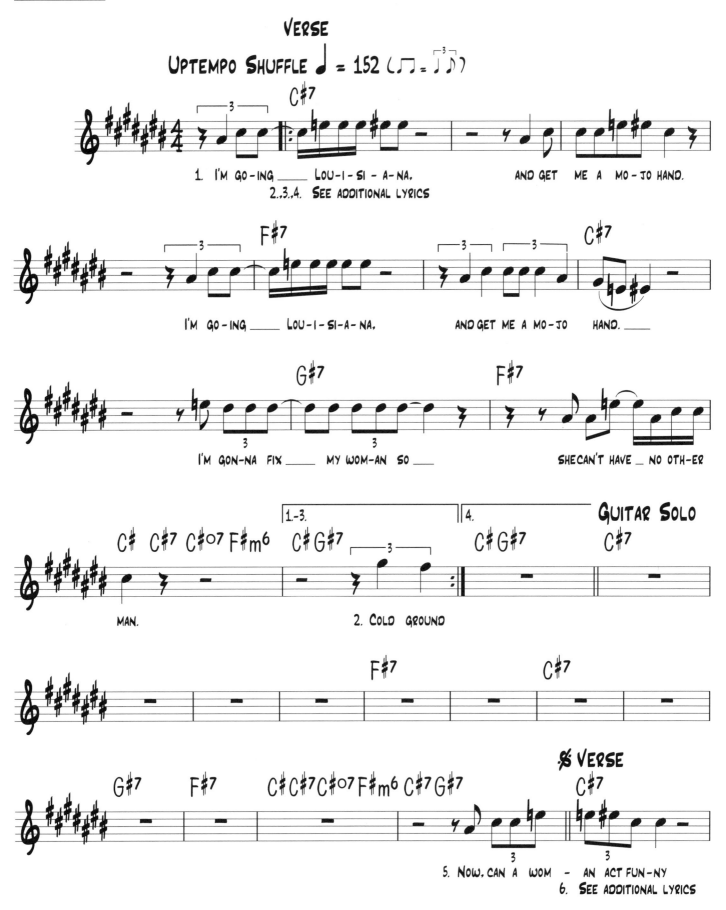

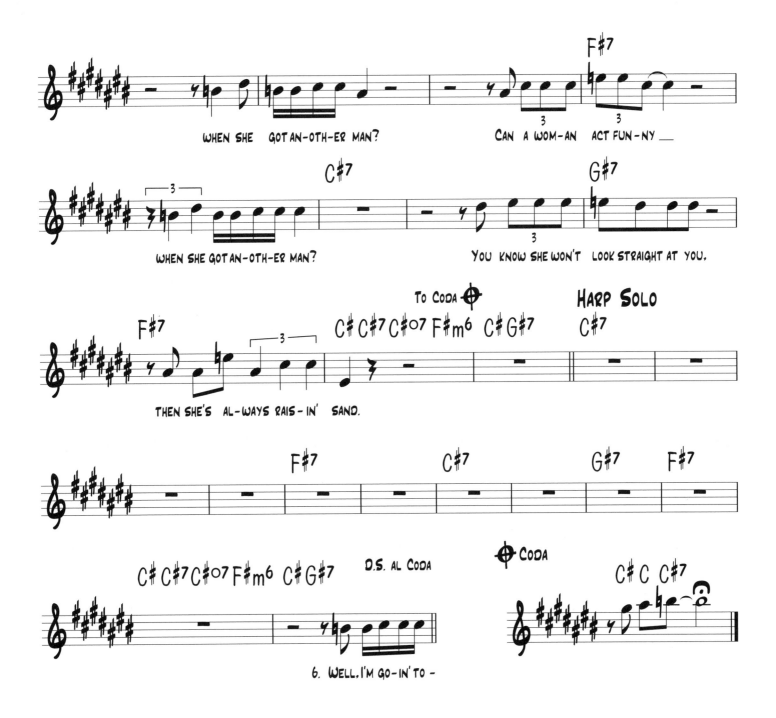

Additional Lyrics

2. Cold ground was my bed last night, rocks was my pillow, too.
   Cold ground was my bed last night, rocks was my pillow, too.
   I woke up this mornin', I wondered, "What in the world am I gonna do?"

3. I lay down thinkin', "Buy me a mojo hand."
   I lay down thinkin', "Buy me a mojo hand."
   I just wanna fix my woman so she can't have no other man.

4. But don't let your woman fix you like mine fixed me.
   Don't let your woman, boy, fix you like mine fixed me.
   She make a fool about her, about as a fool can be.

6. Well, I'm goin' tomorrow, but I won't be gone long.
   I'm goin' tomorrow, but I won't be gone very long.
   I'm gonna get me a mojo hand, I'm gonna bring it back home.

OKIE DOKIE STOMP

WORDS AND MUSIC BY PLUMMER "IVORY" DAVIS

FAST BLUES SHUFFLE ♩ = 182

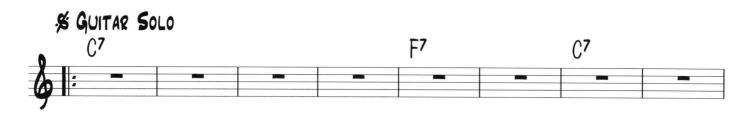

Guitar Solo

To CODA

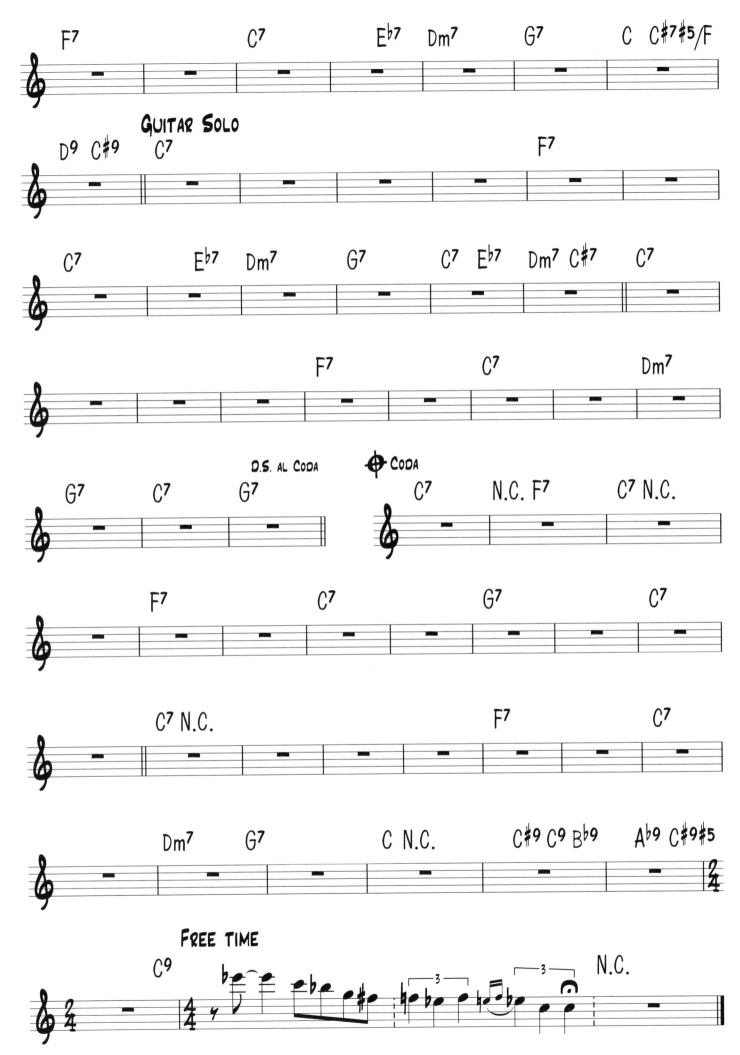

Pride and Joy

Written by Stevie Ray Vaughan

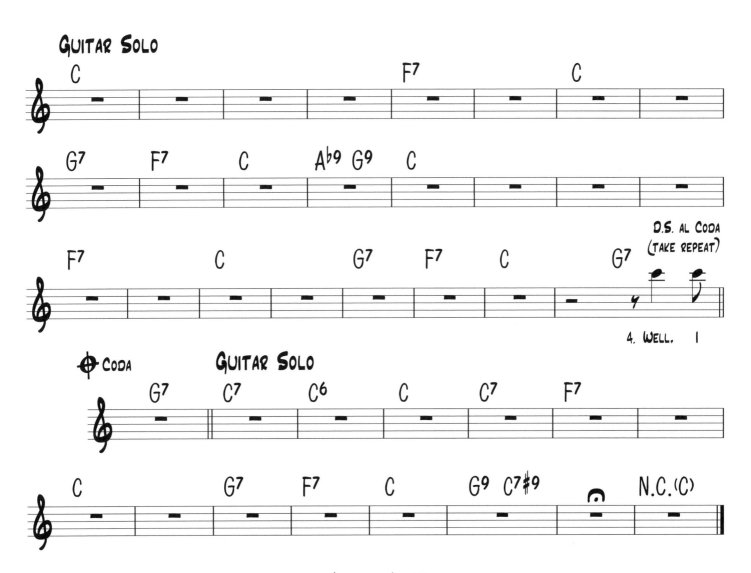

Additional Lyrics

2. Yeah, I love my baby, my heart and soul.
   Love like ours ah, won't never grow old.
   She('s) me sweet little thang,
   She('s) my pride and joy.
   She('s) my sweet little baby,
   I'm her little lover boy.

3. Yeah, I love my lady to be long and lean.
   You mess with her, you'll see a man gettin' mean.
   She('s) my sweet little thang,
   She('s) my pride and joy.
   She('s) my sweet little baby,
   I'm her little lover boy.

4. Well, I love my baby like the finest w. wine.
   Stick with her until the end of time.
   An' she's my sweet little thang,
   She('s) my pride and joy.
   She('s) my sweet little baby,
   I'm her little lover boy.

5. Yeah, I love my baby, my heart and soul.
   Love like ours ah, won't never grow old.
   She('s) my sweet little thang,
   She('s) my pride and joy.
   She('s) my sweet little baby,
   I'm her little lover boy.

RECONSIDER BABY

WORDS AND MUSIC BY LOWELL FULSON

INTRO-SOLO
MODERATE SHUFFLE ♩ = 96

1. So

.𝄋 VERSE

LONG,_____

2., 3. SEE ADDITIONAL LYRICS

OH, HOW I HATE __ TO SEE YOU GO.

SO LONG. _____

OH, HOW I HATE __ TO SEE YOU

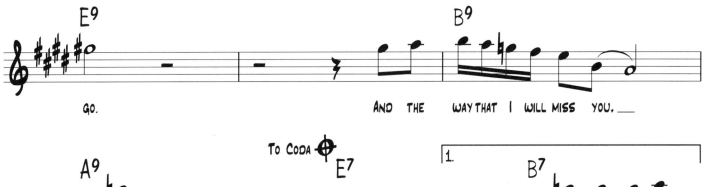

GO.

AND THE WAY THAT I WILL MISS YOU. __

I GUESS YOU WILL NEV - ER KNOW.

2. WE'VE BEEN TO-GETH-

HARP/GUITAR SOLOS

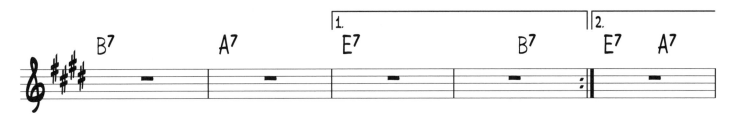

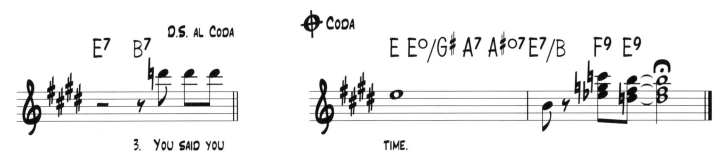

3. YOU SAID YOU

TIME.

ADDITIONAL LYRICS

2. WE'VE BEEN TOGETHER SO LONG TO HAVE TO SEPARATE THIS WAY.
   WE'VE BEEN TOGETHER SO LONG TO HAVE TO SEPARATE THIS WAY.
   I'M GONNA LET YOU GO AHEAD ON, BABY, PRAY THAT YOU'LL COME BACK HOME SOME DAY.

3. YOU SAID YOU ONCE HAD LOVED ME, BUT NOW I GUESS YOU HAVE CHANGED YOUR MIND.
   YOU SAID YOU ONCE HAD LOVED ME, BUT NOW I GUESS YOU HAVE CHANGED YOUR MIND.
   WHY DON'T YOU RECONSIDER, BABY, GIVE YOURSELF JUST A LITTLE MORE TIME.

T-Bone Shuffle
By T-Bone Walker

INTRO
UPTEMPO SHUFFLE ♩ = 138

HARP/GUITAR SOLOS

Additional Lyrics

2. You can't take it with you, that's one thing for sure.
You can't take it with you, that's one thing for sure.
There's nothing wrong with you that a good shuffle boogie won't cure.

3. Have your fun while you can, fate's an awful thing.
Have your fun while you can, fate's an awful thing.
You can't tell what might happen, that's why I love to sing.

The Things That I Used to Do

Words and Music by Eddie "Guitar Slim" Jones

Guitar Solo

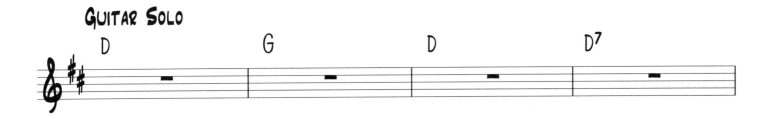

D.S. AL CODA

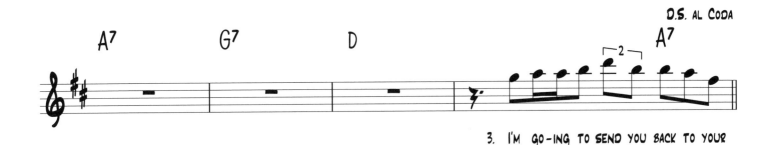

3. I'M GO-ING TO SEND YOU BACK TO YOUR

CODA
OUTRO
STRAIGHT 8THS

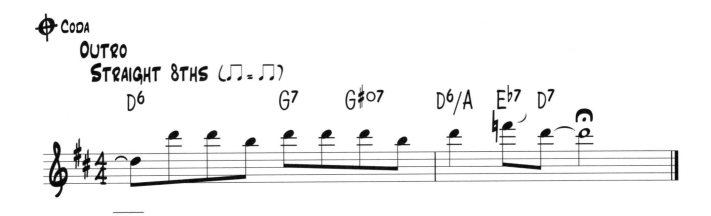

ADDITIONAL LYRICS

2. I WOULD SEARCH ALL NIGHT FOR YOU, BABY,
   LORD, AND MY SEARCH WOULD ALWAYS END IN VAIN.
   I WOULD SEARCH ALL NIGHT FOR YOU, BABY,
   LORD, AND MY SEARCH WOULD ALWAYS END IN VAIN.
   BUT I KNEW ALL ALONG, DARLIN',
   THAT YOU WAS HID OUT WITH YOUR OTHER MAN.

3. I'M GOING TO SEND YOU BACK TO YOUR MOTHER, BABY,
   LORD, AND I'M GOING BACK TO MY FAMILY, TOO.
   I'M GOING TO SEND YOU BACK TO YOUR MOTHER, BABY,
   LORD, AND I'M GOING BACK TO MY FAMILY, TOO.
   'CAUSE NOTHIN' I DO THAT PLEASE YOU, BABY,
   LORD, I JUST CAN'T GET ALONG WITH YOU.

𝄢 **C Version**

Hide Away

By Freddie King and Sonny Thompson

Medium Fast Shuffle ♩ = 138

STRAIGHT 8THS (♩♩ = ♩♩)

D.S. AL CODA

⊕ CODA **STRAIGHT 8THS** (♩♩ = ♩♩)

CD TRACK
② Full Stereo Mix
⑩ Split Mix
𝄢 C Version

If You Love Me Like You Say

Words and Music by Little Johnny Taylor

Intro
Moderate Funk ♩ = 116

ROUND. BA - BY.   SAID YOU'D NEV-ER STAY OUT   LATE.   LET ME TELL YOU, PERT-TY

D.S. AL CODA 1

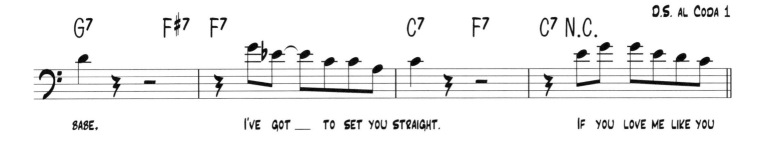

BABE.   I'VE GOT __ TO SET YOU STRAIGHT.   IF YOU LOVE ME LIKE YOU

Coda 1

GUITAR/HARP SOLOS

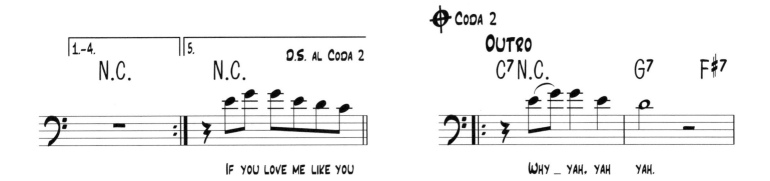

IF YOU LOVE ME LIKE YOU

Coda 2

OUTRO

WHY _ YAH. YAH   YAH.

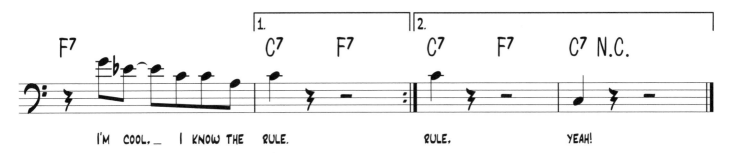

I'M COOL. __ I KNOW THE RULE.   RULE,   YEAH!

Mojo Hand

Words and Music by
Morris Levy, Sam Hopkins and Clarence L. Lewis

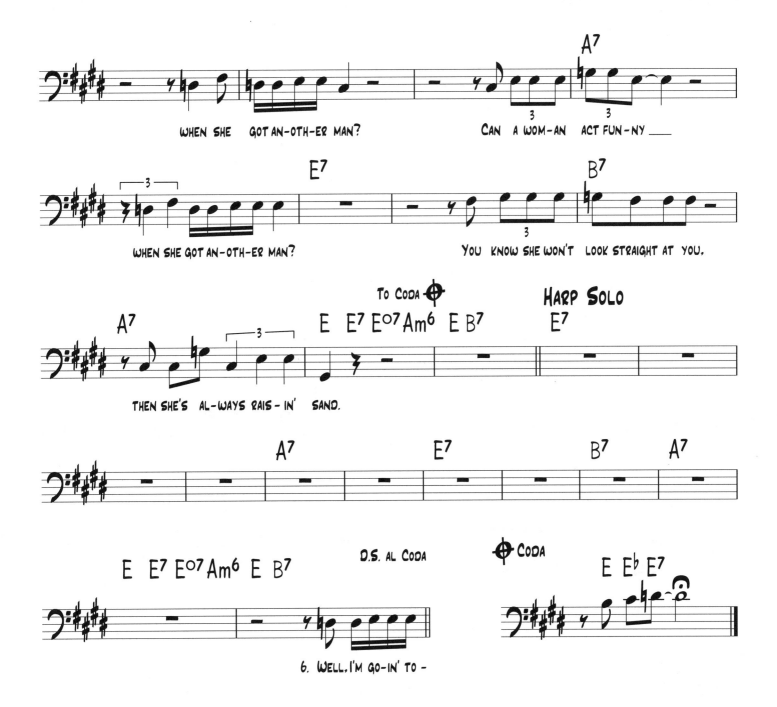

Additional Lyrics

2. Cold ground was my bed last night, rocks was my pillow, too.
   Cold ground was my bed last night, rocks was my pillow, too.
   I woke up this mornin', I wondered, "What in the world am I gonna do?"

3. I lay down thinkin', "Buy me a mojo hand."
   I lay down thinkin', "Buy me a mojo hand."
   I just wanna fix my woman so she can't have no other man.

4. But don't let your woman fix you like mine fixed me.
   Don't let your woman, boy, fix you like mine fixed me.
   She make a fool about her, about as a fool can be.

6. Well, I'm goin' tomorrow, but I won't be gone long.
   I'm goin' tomorrow, but I won't be gone very long.
   I'm gonna get me a mojo hand, I'm gonna bring it back home.

Okie Dokie Stomp

Words and Music by Plummer "Ivory" Davis

Fast Blues Shuffle ♩ = 182 (♫ = ♩♪)

𝄋 Guitar Solo

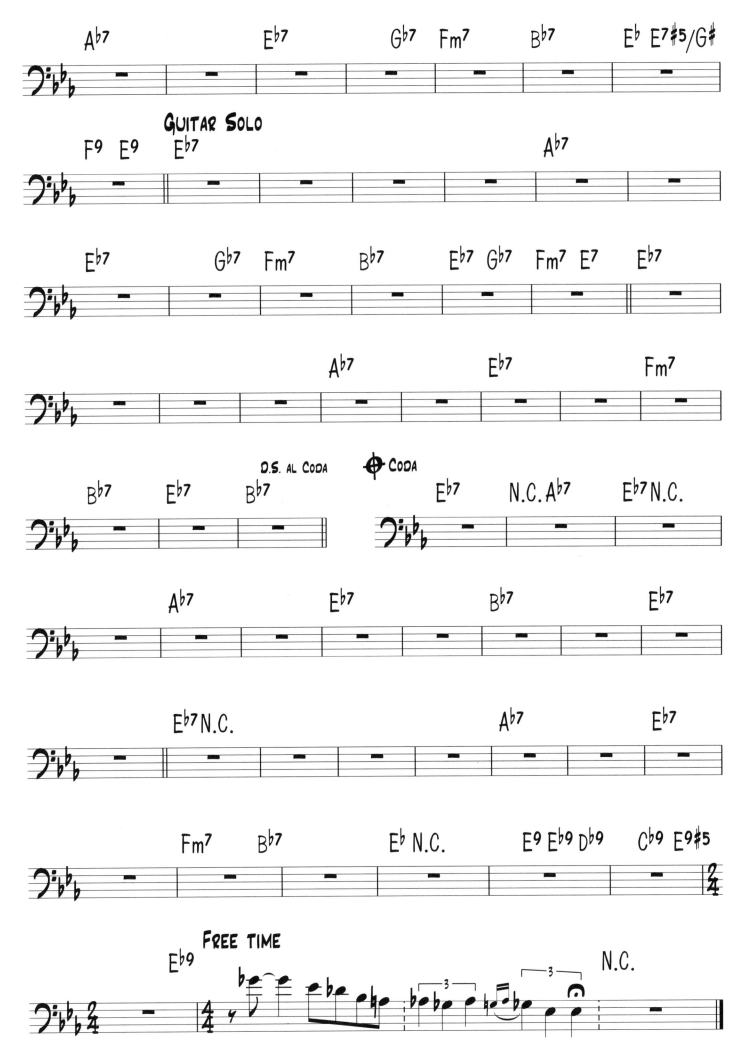

Pride and Joy

Written by Stevie Ray Vaughan

INTRO
MODERATE SHUFFLE ♩ = 122

Additional Lyrics

2. Yeah, I love my baby, my heart and soul.
   Love like ours ah, won't never grow old.
   She('s) me sweet little thang,
   She('s) my pride and joy.
   She('s) my sweet little baby,
   I'm her little lover boy.

3. Yeah, I love my lady to be long and lean,
   You mess with her, you'll see a man gettin' mean.
   She('s) my sweet little thang,
   She('s) my pride and joy.
   She('s) my sweet little baby,
   I'm her little lover boy.

4. Well, I love my baby like the finest w, wine.
   Stick with her until the end of time.
   An' she's my sweet little thang,
   She('s) my pride and joy.
   She('s) my sweet little baby,
   I'm her little lover boy.

5. Yeah, I love my baby, my heart and soul.
   Love like ours ah, won't never grow old.
   She('s) my sweet little thang,
   She('s) my pride and joy.
   She('s) my sweet little baby,
   I'm her little lover boy.

Reconsider Baby

Words and Music by Lowell Fulson

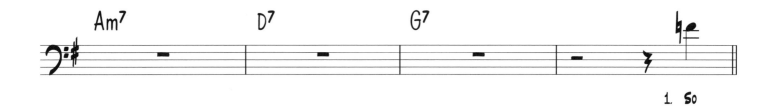

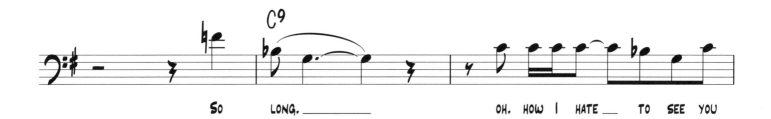

GO. AND THE WAY THAT I WILL MISS YOU, ___

I GUESS YOU WILL NEV - ER KNOW. 2. WE'VE BEEN TO-GETH-

Harp/Guitar Solos

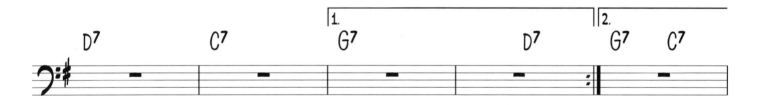

3. YOU SAID YOU TIME.

Additional Lyrics

2. We've been together so long to have to separate this way.
We've been together so long to have to separate this way.
I'm gonna let you go ahead on, baby, pray that you'll come back home some day.

3. You said you once had loved me, but now I guess you have changed your mind.
You said you once had loved me, but now I guess you have changed your mind.
Why don't you reconsider, baby, give yourself just a little more time.

T-Bone Shuffle
By T-Bone Walker

INTRO
UPTEMPO SHUFFLE ♩ = 138

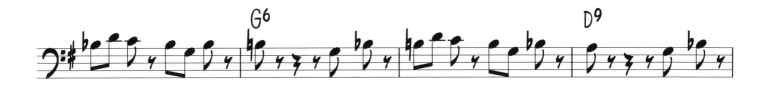

HARP/GUITAR SOLOS

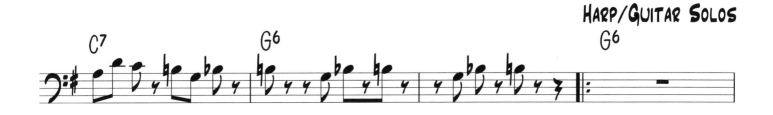

Additional Lyrics

2. You can't take it with you, that's one thing for sure.
    You can't take it with you, that's one thing for sure.
    There's nothing wrong with you that a good shuffle boogie won't cure.

3. Have your fun while you can, fate's an awful thing.
    Have your fun while you can, fate's an awful thing.
    You can't tell what might happen, that's why I love to sing.

The Things That I Used to Do

Words and Music by Eddie "Guitar Slim" Jones

GUITAR SOLO

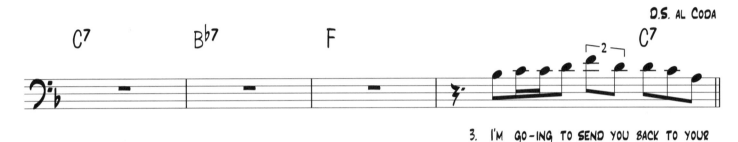

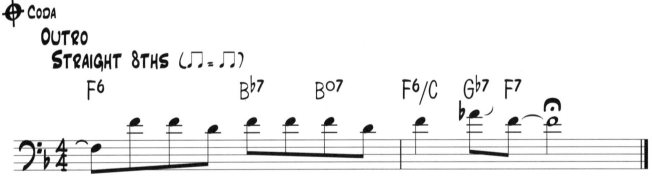

3. I'M GO-ING TO SEND YOU BACK TO YOUR

ADDITIONAL LYRICS

2. I WOULD SEARCH ALL NIGHT FOR YOU, BABY,
   LORD, AND MY SEARCH WOULD ALWAYS END IN VAIN.
   I WOULD SEARCH ALL NIGHT FOR YOU, BABY,
   LORD, AND MY SEARCH WOULD ALWAYS END IN VAIN.
   BUT I KNEW ALL ALONG, DARLIN',
   THAT YOU WAS HID OUT WITH YOUR OTHER MAN.

3. I'M GOING TO SEND YOU BACK TO YOUR MOTHER, BABY,
   LORD, AND I'M GOING BACK TO MY FAMILY, TOO.
   I'M GOING TO SEND YOU BACK TO YOUR MOTHER, BABY,
   LORD, AND I'M GOING BACK TO MY FAMILY, TOO.
   'CAUSE NOTHIN' I DO THAT PLEASE YOU, BABY,
   LORD, I JUST CAN'T GET ALONG WITH YOU.

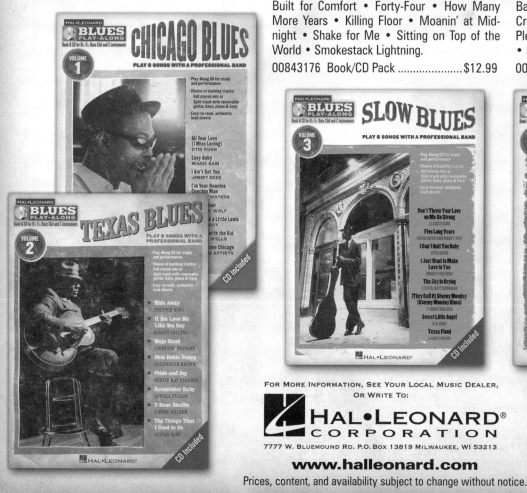

Jazz Instruction & Improvisation
Books for All Instruments from Hal Leonard

AN APPROACH TO JAZZ IMPROVISATION
by Dave Pozzi
Musicians Institute Press
Explore the styles of Charlie Parker, Sonny Rollins, Bud Powell and others with this comprehensive guide to jazz improvisation. Covers: scale choices • chord analysis • phrasing • melodies • harmonic progressions • more.
00695135 Book/CD Pack $17.95

BUILDING A JAZZ VOCABULARY
By Mike Steinel
A valuable resource for learning the basics of jazz from Mike Steinel of the University of North Texas. It covers: the basics of jazz • how to build effective solos • a comprehensive practice routine • and a jazz vocabulary of the masters.
00849911 ....$19.95

THE CYCLE OF FIFTHS
by Emile and Laura De Cosmo
This essential instruction book provides more than 450 exercises, including hundreds of melodic and rhythmic ideas. The book is designed to help improvisors master the cycle of fifths, one of the primary progressions in music. Guaranteed to refine technique, enhance improvisational fluency, and improve sight-reading!
00311114 ....$16.99

THE DIATONIC CYCLE
by Emile and Laura De Cosmo
Renowned jazz educators Emile and Laura De Cosmo provide more than 300 exercises to help improvisors tackle one of music's most common progressions: the diatonic cycle. This book is guaranteed to refine technique, enhance improvisational fluency, and improve sight-reading!
00311115 ....$16.95

EAR TRAINING
by Keith Wyatt,
Carl Schroeder and Joe Elliott
Musicians Institute Press
Covers: basic pitch matching • singing major and minor scales • identifying intervals • transcribing melodies and rhythm • identifying chords and progressions • seventh chords and the blues • modal interchange, chromaticism, modulation • and more.
00695198 Book/2-CD Pack $24.95

EXERCISES AND ETUDES FOR THE JAZZ INSTRUMENTALIST
by J.J. Johnson
Designed as study material and playable by any instrument, these pieces run the gamut of the jazz experience, featuring common and uncommon time signatures and keys, and styles from ballads to funk. They are progressively graded so that both beginners and professionals will be challenged by the demands of this wonderful music.
00842018 Bass Clef Edition $16.95
00842042 Treble Clef Edition $16.95

JAZZOLOGY
THE ENCYCLOPEDIA OF JAZZ THEORY FOR ALL MUSICIANS
by Robert Rawlins and Nor Eddine Bahha
This comprehensive resource covers a variety of jazz topics, for beginners and pros of any instrument. The book serves as an encyclopedia for reference, a thorough methodology for the student, and a workbook for the classroom.
00311167 ....$18.95

JAZZ JAM SESSION
15 TRACKS INCLUDING RHYTHM CHANGES, BLUES, BOSSA, BALLADS & MORE
by Ed Friedland
Bring your local jazz jam session home! These essential jazz rhythm grooves feature a professional rhythm section and are perfect for guitar, harmonica, keyboard, saxophone and trumpet players to hone their soloing skills. The feels, tempos and keys have been varied to broaden your jazz experience. Styles include: ballads, bebop, blues, bossa nova, cool jazz, and more, with improv guidelines for each track.
00311827 Book/CD Pack $19.99

JAZZ THEORY RESOURCES
by Bert Ligon
Houston Publishing, Inc.
This is a jazz theory text in two volumes. **Volume 1 includes:** review of basic theory • rhythm in jazz performance • triadic generalization • diatonic harmonic progressions and analysis • substitutions and turnarounds • and more. **Volume 2 includes:** modes and modal frameworks • quartal harmony • extended tertian structures and triadic superimposition • pentatonic applications • coloring "outside" the lines and beyond • and more.
00030458 Volume 1 ....$39.95
00030459 Volume 2 ....$29.95

JOY OF IMPROV
by Dave Frank and John Amaral
This book/CD course on improvisation for all instruments and all styles will help players develop monster musical skills! **Book One** imparts a solid basis in technique, rhythm, chord theory, ear training and improv concepts. **Book Two** explores more advanced chord voicings, chord arranging techniques and more challenging blues and melodic lines. The CD can be used as a listening and play-along tool.
00220005 Book 1 – Book/CD Pack $27.99
00220006 Book 2 – Book/CD Pack $24.95

THE PATH TO JAZZ IMPROVISATION
by Emile and Laura De Cosmo
This fascinating jazz instruction book offers an innovative, scholarly approach to the art of improvisation. It includes in-depth analysis and lessons about: cycle of fifths • diatonic cycle • overtone series • pentatonic scale • harmonic and melodic minor scale • polytonal order of keys • blues and bebop scales • modes • and more.
00310904 ....$14.95

THE SOURCE
THE DICTIONARY OF CONTEMPORARY AND TRADITIONAL SCALES
by Steve Barta
This book serves as an informative guide for people who are looking for good, solid information regarding scales, chords, and how they work together. It provides right and left hand fingerings for scales, chords, and complete inversions. Includes over 20 different scales, each written in all 12 keys.
00240885 ....$15.95

21 BEBOP EXERCISES
by Steve Rawlins
This book/CD pack is both a warm-up collection and a manual for bebop phrasing. Its tasty and sophisticated exercises will help you develop your proficiency with jazz interpretation. It concentrates on practice in all twelve keys – moving higher by half-step – to help develop dexterity and range. The companion CD includes all of the exercises in 12 keys.
00315341 Book/CD Pack $17.95

Prices, contents & availability subject to change without notice.

Visit Hal Leonard online at
www.halleonard.com

0910

For use with all B-flat, E-flat, Bass Clef and C instruments, the Jazz Play-Along® Series is the ultimate learning tool for all jazz musicians. With musician-friendly lead sheets, melody cues, and other split-track choices on the included CD, these first-of-a-kind packages help you master improvisation while playing some of the greatest tunes of all time. FOR STUDY, each tune includes a split track with: melody cue with proper style and inflection • professional rhythm tracks • choruses for soloing • removable bass part • removable piano part. FOR PERFORMANCE, each tune also has: an additional full stereo accompaniment track (no melody) • additional choruses for soloing.

1. DUKE ELLINGTON
00841644......................$16.95

1A. MAIDEN VOYAGE/ALL BLUES
00843158 ....$15.99

2. MILES DAVIS
00841645......................$16.95

3. THE BLUES
00841646......................$16.99

4. JAZZ BALLADS
00841691......................$16.99

5. BEST OF BEBOP
00841689......................$16.95

6. JAZZ CLASSICS WITH EASY CHANGES
00841690......................$16.99

7. ESSENTIAL JAZZ STANDARDS
00843000......................$16.99

8. ANTONIO CARLOS JOBIM AND THE ART OF THE BOSSA NOVA
00843001......................$16.95

9. DIZZY GILLESPIE
00843002......................$16.99

10. DISNEY CLASSICS
00843003......................$16.99

11. RODGERS AND HART FAVORITES
00843004......................$16.99

12. ESSENTIAL JAZZ CLASSICS
00843005......................$16.99

13. JOHN COLTRANE
00843006......................$16.95

14. IRVING BERLIN
00843007......................$15.99

15. RODGERS & HAMMERSTEIN
00843008......................$15.99

16. COLE PORTER
00843009......................$15.95

17. COUNT BASIE
00843010......................$16.95

18. HAROLD ARLEN
00843011......................$15.95

19. COOL JAZZ
00843012......................$15.95

20. CHRISTMAS CAROLS
00843080......................$14.95

21. RODGERS AND HART CLASSICS
00843014......................$14.95

22. WAYNE SHORTER
00843015......................$16.95

23. LATIN JAZZ
00843016......................$16.95

24. EARLY JAZZ STANDARDS
00843017......................$14.95

25. CHRISTMAS JAZZ
00843018......................$16.95

26. CHARLIE PARKER
00843019......................$16.95

27. GREAT JAZZ STANDARDS
00843020......................$16.99

28. BIG BAND ERA
00843021......................$15.99

29. LENNON AND MCCARTNEY
00843022......................$16.95

30. BLUES' BEST
00843023......................$15.99

31. JAZZ IN THREE
00843024......................$15.99

32. BEST OF SWING
00843025......................$15.99

33. SONNY ROLLINS
00843029......................$15.95

34. ALL TIME STANDARDS
00843030......................$15.99

35. BLUESY JAZZ
00843031......................$16.99

36. HORACE SILVER
00843032......................$16.99

37. BILL EVANS
00843033......................$16.95

38. YULETIDE JAZZ
00843034......................$16.95

39. "ALL THE THINGS YOU ARE" & MORE JEROME KERN SONGS
00843035......................$15.99

40. BOSSA NOVA
00843036......................$15.99

41. CLASSIC DUKE ELLINGTON
00843037......................$16.99

42. GERRY MULLIGAN FAVORITES
00843038......................$16.99

43. GERRY MULLIGAN CLASSICS
00843039......................$16.95

44. OLIVER NELSON
00843040......................$16.95

45. JAZZ AT THE MOVIES
00843041......................$15.99

46. BROADWAY JAZZ STANDARDS
00843042......................$15.99

47. CLASSIC JAZZ BALLADS
00843043......................$15.99

48. BEBOP CLASSICS
00843044......................$16.99

49. MILES DAVIS STANDARDS
00843045......................$16.95

50. GREAT JAZZ CLASSICS
00843046......................$15.99

51. UP-TEMPO JAZZ
00843047......................$15.99

52. STEVIE WONDER
00843048......................$16.99

53. RHYTHM CHANGES
00843049......................$15.99

54. "MOONLIGHT IN VERMONT" AND OTHER GREAT STANDARDS
00843050......................$15.99

55. BENNY GOLSON
00843052......................$15.95

56. "GEORGIA ON MY MIND" & OTHER SONGS BY HOAGY CARMICHAEL
00843056 ....$15.99

57. VINCE GUARALDI
00843057......................$16.99

58. MORE LENNON AND MCCARTNEY
00843059......................$15.99

59. SOUL JAZZ
00843060.....................................$15.99

60. DEXTER GORDON
00843061.....................................$15.95

61. MONGO SANTAMARIA
00843062.....................................$15.95

62. JAZZ-ROCK FUSION
00843063.....................................$16.99

63. CLASSICAL JAZZ
00843064.....................................$14.95

64. TV TUNES
00843065.....................................$14.95

65. SMOOTH JAZZ
00843066.....................................$16.99

66. A CHARLIE BROWN CHRISTMAS
00843067.....................................$16.99

67. CHICK COREA
00843068.....................................$15.95

68. CHARLES MINGUS
00843069.....................................$16.95

69. CLASSIC JAZZ
00843071.....................................$15.99

70. THE DOORS
00843072.....................................$14.95

71. COLE PORTER CLASSICS
00843073.....................................$14.95

72. CLASSIC JAZZ BALLADS
00843074.....................................$15.99

73. JAZZ/BLUES
00843075 ....$14.95

74. BEST JAZZ CLASSICS
00843076 ....$15.99

75. PAUL DESMOND
00843077 ....$14.95

76. BROADWAY JAZZ BALLADS
00843078 ....$15.99

77. JAZZ ON BROADWAY
00843079 ....$15.99

78. STEELY DAN
00843070 ....$14.99

79. MILES DAVIS CLASSICS
00843081 ....$15.99

80. JIMI HENDRIX
00843083 ....$15.99

81. FRANK SINATRA – CLASSICS
00843084.....................................$15.99

82. FRANK SINATRA – STANDARDS
00843085 ....$15.99

83. ANDREW LLOYD WEBBER
00843104 ....$14.95

84. BOSSA NOVA CLASSICS
00843105 ....$14.95

85. MOTOWN HITS
00843109 ....$14.95

86. BENNY GOODMAN
00843110 ....$14.95

87. DIXIELAND
00843111 ....$14.95

88. DUKE ELLINGTON FAVORITES
00843112 ....$14.95

89. IRVING BERLIN FAVORITES
00843113 ....$14.95

90. THELONIOUS MONK CLASSICS
00841262 ....$16.99

91. THELONIOUS MONK FAVORITES
00841263 ....$16.99

92. LEONARD BERNSTEIN
00450134 ....$15.99

93. DISNEY FAVORITES
00843142 ....$14.99

94. RAY
00843143 ....$14.99

95. JAZZ AT THE LOUNGE
00843144 ....$14.99

96. LATIN JAZZ STANDARDS
00843145 ....$14.99

97. MAYBE I'M AMAZED
00843148 ....$15.99

98. DAVE FRISHBERG
00843149 ....$15.99

99. SWINGING STANDARDS
00843150 ....$14.99

100. LOUIS ARMSTRONG
00740423 ....$15.99

101. BUD POWELL
00843152 ....$14.99

102. JAZZ POP
00843153 ....$14.99

103. ON GREEN DOLPHIN STREET & OTHER JAZZ CLASSICS
00843154 ....$14.99

104. ELTON JOHN
00843155 ....$14.99

105. SOULFUL JAZZ
00843151 ....$15.99

106. SLO' JAZZ
00843117 ....$14.99

107. MOTOWN CLASSICS
00843116 ....$14.99

108. JAZZ WALTZ
00843159 ....$15.99

109. OSCAR PETERSON
00843160 ....$16.99

110. JUST STANDARDS
00843161 ....$15.99

111. COOL CHRISTMAS
00843162 ....$15.99

112. PAQUITO D'RIVERA – LATIN JAZZ
48020662 ....$16.99

113. PAQUITO D'RIVERA – BRAZILIAN JAZZ
48020663 ....$19.99

114. MODERN JAZZ QUARTET FAVORITES
00843163 ....$15.99

115. THE SOUND OF MUSIC
00843164 ....$15.99

116. JACO PASTORIUS
00843165 ....$15.99

117. ANTONIO CARLOS JOBIM – MORE HITS
00843166 ....$15.99

118. BIG JAZZ STANDARDS COLLECTION
00843167 ....$27.50

119. JELLY ROLL MORTON
00843168 ....$15.99

120. J.S. BACH
00843169 ....$15.99

121. DJANGO REINHARDT
00843170 ....$15.99

122. PAUL SIMON
00843182 ....$16.99

123. BACHARACH & DAVID
00843185 ....$15.99

124. JAZZ-ROCK HORN HITS
00843186 ....$15.99

126. COUNT BASIE CLASSICS
00843157 ....$15.99

127. CHUCK MANGIONE
00843188 ....$15.99

132. STAN GETZ ESSENTIALS
00843193 ....$15.99

133. STAN GETZ FAVORITES
00843194 ....$15.99

135. JEFF BECK
00843197 ....$15.99

137. WES MONTGOMERY
00843199 ....$15.99

139. JULIAN "CANNONBALL" ADDERLEY
00843201 ....$15.99

150. JAZZ IMPROV BASICS
00843195 ....$19.99

Prices, contents, and availability subject to change without notice.

FOR MORE INFORMATION,
SEE YOUR LOCAL MUSIC DEALER,
OR WRITE TO:

HAL•LEONARD®
CORPORATION
7777 W. BLUEMOUND RD. P.O. BOX 13819
MILWAUKEE, WISCONSIN 53213
For complete songlists and more,
visit Hal Leonard online at
www.halleonard.com

0311